absolute MAUI

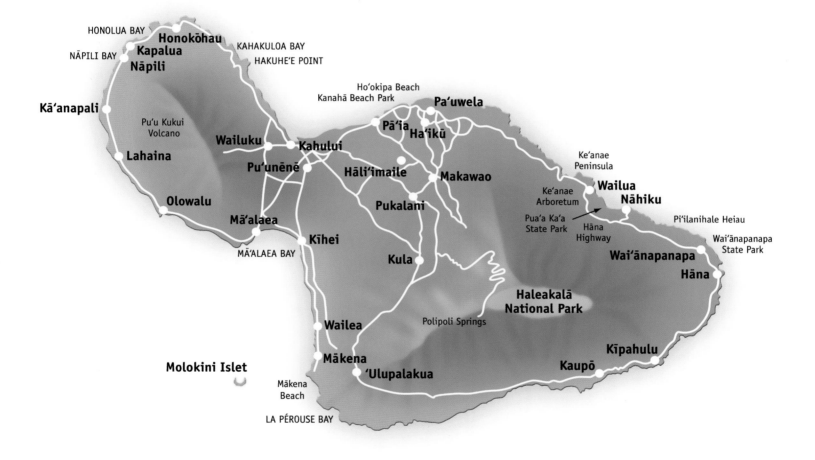

HONOLUA BAY

Honokōhau

KAHAKULOA BAY

NĀPILI BAY **Kapalua**

Nāpili

HAKUHE'E POINT

Ho'okipa Beach

Kanahā Beach Park

Pa'uwela

Kā'anapali

Pu'u Kukui
Volcano

Wailuku

Pā'ia **Ha'ikū**

Kahului

Ke'anae
Peninsula

Lahaina

Pu'unēnē

Hāli'imaile

Makawao

Ke'anae
Arboretum

Wailua

Nāhiku

Olowalu

Pukalani

Pua'a Ka'a
State Park

Hāna
Highway

Pi'ilanihale Heiau

Mā'alaea

Wai'ānapanapa
State Park

Kīhei

MĀ'ALAEA BAY

Kula

Wai'ānapanapa

Hāna

Wailea

Polipoli Springs

**Haleakalā
National Park**

Molokini Islet

Mākena

Kīpahulu

'Ulupalakua

Kaupō

Mākena
Beach

LA PÉROUSE BAY

FACTS ABOUT MAUI

Square miles: 729   Acres: 466,304   Length: 48 miles   Width: 26 miles   Population: 147,000 (2010)

Distance from Honolulu: 70 miles   Distance from San Francisco: 2,390 miles   Highest point: Haleakalā Summit 10,023 feet

absolute
MAUI

—⌒—

FEATURING THE IMAGES OF
MAUI'S FINEST PHOTOGRAPHERS

BOB BANGERTER   RANDY JAY BRAUN   CINDY CAMPBELL

RON DAHLQUIST   ROB DECAMP   QUINCY DEIN   TERRIE ELIKER

DAVID FLEETHAM   ANITA HARRIS   DOUGLAS J. HOFFMAN   AUBREY HORD

RANDY HUFFORD   LEAH MARK   LAURENT MARTRES

SCOTT MEAD   LINNY MORRIS   MIKE NEAL   CAMERON NELSON

TONY NOVAK-CLIFFORD   DAVID OLSEN   DOUGLAS PEEBLES

ZACH PEZZILLO   DAVE SCHOONOVER   MONICA & MICHAEL SWEET

SHANE TEGARDEN   GREG VAUGHN   JESSICA VELTRI   DAVID WATERSUN

FRANK WICKER   MARTY WOLFF   DARRELL WONG

This page: A fish-eye lens captures a pair of humpback whales surfacing through clear Maui waters for a "spy hop" or short look around. Photo © Marty Wolff.
Opposite: A rare "south swell" explodes off a black lava headland and thunders across the reef near La Pérouse Bay. Photo © David Schoonover. **Preceding spread, left:** Wailua Falls is one of Maui's most beautiful and accessible. It is right next to the Hāna Road near mile marker 45. Photo © Jessica Veltri.

absolute
MAUI

PHOTOGRAPHY EDITED BY DOUGLAS PEEBLES

WRITTEN BY TOM STEVENS

Backlit by fiery clouds and a satiny sea, hula dancers tread cool sands at the margin of a Maui day. Photo © David Olsen.

absolute
MAUI

PHOTOGRAPHY EDITED BY DOUGLAS PEEBLES

WRITTEN BY TOM STEVENS

DESIGN BY NANCY WATANABE

Table of Contents

ISBN-10: 1-56647-959-2
ISBN 13: 978-1-56647-959-2
Library of Congress Control Number: 2011935677

Design by Nancy Watanabe

First Printing, October 2011

Mutual Publishing, LLC
1215 Center Street, Suite 210
Honolulu, Hawai'i 96816
Ph: (808) 732-1709
Fax: (808) 734-4094
e-mail: info@mutualpublishing.com
www.mutualpublishing.com

Printed in China

Preface

Absolute Maui started out as a new edition of *Maui On My Mind,* which, over its almost twenty-five year life beginning in 1985, had become a Maui icon. But difficulties arose immediately. On closer scrutiny, most of the photos had become dated (except for the underwater and flower photography.) Many scenic views now included man-made environs. Adorable kids had become adults, some with kids of their own. Styles and models of cars, clothes and other things had changed. And sugar, macadamia nut and pineapple fields, which once dominated the island, had disappeared with only one sugar mill still operating in 2011. In essence, *Maui On My Mind* was a document of an earlier time now nostalgic—mid-1980s Maui.

As well, a new generation of photographers were shooting Maui, and photography itself had significantly changed becoming mostly digital which opened up a new range of possibilities. Digital's low light ability makes natural-looking, candid, indoor or twilight photography possible where tripods and flashes were needed before, and enables photographers to move around more freely to find the exact perspective from which to shoot. Nor are the number of images shot limited by the film roll. Ocean photographers can now shoot hundreds of photos without reloading, whereas 36 shots was the max before. In landscape photography, the range of shadow to highlight has been dramatically increased, giving a result much closer to what the eye perceives.

As well, marketing specialists had recommended a smaller size book than *Maui On My Mind* because of recent airlines' baggage charges limiting the weight of what visitors can carry back without additional expense, and because younger readers favor digital content rather than physical pages.

We ended up opting for an entirely new book of about the same size with new perspectives. Maui's imagery is too vast, too unusual

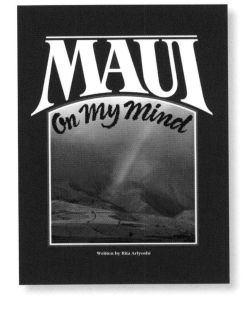

for a smaller book, and the photography being submitted was too strong to limit the number of pages. There was even ample material for a book on each chapter. A new book could also incorporate several important subject themes that had emerged since *Maui On My Mind's* appearance: growing concern over conservation, rising popularity of ocean activity, a vibrant renaissance of the Hawaiian culture and a future based on environmentally friendly technology.

We also decided not to include vintage or nostalgia photos. The generation that would appreciate the old days has almost all passed on. Many of today's Mauians were not born on Maui or have not been residents long enough to appreciate or remember grandparent reminiscences.

As with *Maui On My Mind,* we turned to only Maui photographers (with one or two exceptions) to provide the photography, asking them for images that they felt captured today's Maui. In total, 9,500 images from 50 photographers were reviewed digitally. Then began the most difficult task to narrow down the number resulting in the 175 images from thirty-two photographers that appear in the following pages. We are sure you will agree with our decision to produce an entirely new book.

Many helped. Those on stage—the designer, the writer, and the photo editor are credited on the title pages and on the dustjacket. The pages that follow are a testament to their ability and achievement. Appearing on the closing pages are brief biographies of the photographers, without whom *Absolute Maui* would not have been possible and whose skill enables a work of this scope.

Behind the scenes, valuable assistance was provided by Mutual Publishing's Kaylen Baker, Jane Gillespie, Erika Roberts, Gay Wong, and Courtney Young. Keli'i Brown and Lynn Erfer of the Maui Visitors Bureau shared their thoughts as to what impresses visitors (scenery, beaches, Hawaiian people and food), and Karee Carlucci of the Maui Arts and Cultural Center was generous with her insights.

Above: *Maui On My Mind* captured mid-1980s Maui at a time when the island had become a major travel destination, underpopulation was being mentioned, the Hawaiian Renaissance/Sovereignty movement was embryonic, and the plantation era had entered its final years. *Absolute Maui* continues its fine coffee table tradition moving ahead to early 21st century at a time when Maui is still beautiful and alluring (but being challenged), its diverse and expanded population is devoted to its island lifestyle and the surrounding waters, and the island's host people, the Hawaiians, diligently preserve and protect their culture. **Opposite:** Eons of heavy rain have carved sheer cliffs, lofty valleys and near-vertical falls into Maui's windward slopes. Here passing showers turn one Maui escarpment into a wall of tears. Photo © Scott Mead.

Introduction

Those who live on Maui and those who visit the island share a common bond: they don't want to be anywhere else. Some love the beaches, or the mountains, or the ocean, or the weather. Others cherish the family connections and cultural continuity the island nurtures. Many enjoy Maui's unique, friendly, fun-loving, big-hearted, active and healthful lifestyle. And everyone appreciates the island's robust diversity.

The qualities that make Maui unique and universally loved are captured in the chapters that follow. There is a Maui only the sun, the stars, and the birds could see until recently: rugged cliffs, surf-fringed reefs, hidden waterfalls, and eroded mountain tops. There is a Maui seen from a walker's perspective: misty ocean coves, palm-shaded beaches, dramatic overlooks, smoldering sunsets, and storybook skies vivid with rainbows. There is a nature lover's Maui: tiny insects, birds and mountain ferns, dazzling arrays of tropical flowers, as well as monk seals, great whales, and other sea life. There is Upcountry, a "mountain Maui" of scenic farms and ranches;

and the rugged Hāna Coast, where emerald rain forests meet a sapphire sea. Then there is the Maui most familiar to its longtime residents: famous local eateries, fairs, parades, and beloved island celebrities.

Absolute Maui draws its inspiration from the award-winning books *Maui On My Mind* and *Maui, The Last Hawaiian Place* by Robert Wenkam—both of which are now considered classics. But Maui isn't really timeless, as the island is always changing. Wenkam's 1970 Maui differed from the one explored 15 years later in *Maui on My Mind,* although both faithfully represented their eras. *Absolute Maui* revisits the island many consider the world's finest.

Images were requested from Maui's major photographers, who search its mountains and beaches daily for visual opportunities. From the more than 9,500 photographs submitted, the 175 best were selected to appear in these pages. Each image is a representation of the photographer's sense of wonder. Whether the subject is a whimsical roadside stand, a canoe team, a tropical landscape, or simply Mauians enjoying their island

pleasures and pastimes, what is alluring and unique about Maui shines through.

The images show that Maui is a beautiful place, not only to live or to visit, but also to photograph. The subtle daily changes in light and shadow reveal on film the island's spirit, or mana. The wind, ocean, skies, sand, and wildlife—sometimes gracious and sometimes ferocious—provide endless opportunities to capture the island's soul. The images are also intimate: the viewer is invited to see the subject up close, as the photographer sees it.

Absolute Maui also explores how the island has changed. In photos of wind turbines along Maui's ridges and solar roof collectors, we see 21st-century Maui's commitment to renewable energy. And in images of citizen conservation efforts, we gain a new awareness of the fragility of Maui's ecosystems. There is also a special chapter on Maui's host nation—Mauians of Hawaiian ancestry whose cultural practices are now enjoying a vigorous 21st-century renaissance.

Absolute Maui takes its title from the caliber of its images, which were painstakingly taken by the island's finest photographers, utilizing almost every modern-day photographic technique. The title also reminds us what Maui is, what it offers, and how lucky its residents and visitors are.

—Douglas Peebles

Above: Maui's mayor, Alan Arakawa, is an avid softball player. Here, playing for the Harley's Dragons in the Maui Senior Softball 60+ League, he is apparently ready to steal second base. The senior softball league is a classic island experience. Teams from all islands form leagues, buy uniforms, get sponsors, and travel to tournaments on other islands. They play hard and have a good time after the games. It's mostly about fellowship, but the competitive fires still burn brightly and bragging rights are definitely at stake. **Opposite:** Long a staple of photo books and travel magazines, these scenic West Maui cane fields are no more. When Lahaina's Pioneer Mill went out of business, ten thousand acres of sugar gave way to view homes and small farms. The rainbows are still there, though. Photo © David Olsen.

Maui from the Air

As incoming flights near Maui, air passengers enjoy a panorama once seen only by birds.

Pressing up to the view ports, they watch the island's rugged slopes turn slowly beneath the wings. One side of the cabin sees a cloud-capped mountain; the other, surf-fringed coastline.

As the plane descends, forests, farms and pastures form a patchwork quilt of greens and browns. Soon, scattered buildings appear, then towns and a city, then cars as small as grains of rice.

Sooner than seems possible, the view compresses to sky, red earth and wind-bent sugarcane. Then, ka-whump! The aerial part of the show is over.

At commercial jet velocity, the scene lasts about five minutes. Add another five for the flight out, and you have a ten-minute glimpse of Maui from the air. It's a sensational movie, especially at dawn or dusk. But it's a short one.

To truly savor Maui from the air, it requires other strategies. Commercial, military and plantation pilots aside, the first flyers to truly prolong their Maui air time were hang gliders. Starting in the late 1960s, daredevil pilots began launching their fragile craft on windless mornings from Polipoli Meadows and from the summit of Haleakalā.

To this day, they and their parasailing cousins can be seen looping lazily back and forth over the mountain's broad flank, riding thermals and updrafts into the clouds, sometimes spiraling out over the ocean before swooping in to land on Mākena Beach.

Aloft for an hour or more in the rushing silence, these flyers truly savor Maui from the air. But their window is a narrow one— wind conditions allow only a few launches each winter.

Once tour helicopters reached the island in the late 1970s, the skies opened up. Soon sightseers, photographers, surveyors, realtors, celebrities and marijuana police were zipping and hovering over the entire island.

One enterprising Wailea pilot started a wedding business. Teaming up with a guitar-playing minister, he would fly the bride and groom to a scenic overlook or waterfall, photograph the ceremony, then return them to their resort.

Of the hundreds of thousands who have now seen Maui from the air, photographers have benefited the most. Whether taken from helicopters or from slow-flying propeller planes, their images have changed the way the world sees the island.

Thousand-foot waterfalls, misty hanging valleys and remote jungle pools long hidden from view are now revealed, if not made accessible. The ocean in its myriad colors and moods is dazzling from the air. And Maui's two distinctive summits—Haleakalā and Pu'u Kukui—appear almost unearthly from two miles above.

Even more startling are transient images that only an aerial view can provide: afternoon cloud shadows patterning the cane fields; whales and dolphins traveling in mid-channel; thousands of akule fish forming a sphere as silvery as a planet; herds of white-tail deer crossing a high meadow at dawn.

Of course, it doesn't end there. Now imaging satellites have Maui dialed in as never before. You can zoom in on your favorite beach on GoogleEarth, or see how the island looks from space.

Now that's an aerial view.

Above: A pod of humpback whales travels through warm, shallow waters off Maui's Kā'anapali coast. The whales migrate between Alaska and Hawai'i each year. Photo © Douglas Peebles. **Opposite:** Now mostly submerged, crescent-shaped Molokini Islet was once a cinder cone on distant Haleakalā. Today it is a protected marine wonderland. Photo © Douglas Peebles. **Preceding spread:** Wind, wave, rain and sun have sculpted Maui's northwest coast for eons. Cave-pitted Hakuhe'e Point reveals the erosive artistry of the elements. Photo © Douglas Peebles.

Above: A stone breakwall protects the charter boats, pleasure craft and sightseeing vessels that make Lahaina Harbor a key component of West Maui's economy. Photo © Douglas Peebles. **Opposite:** As loopy as a jungle vine, the amazing Hāna Road snakes along sheer cliffs above a cobalt sea. Generations after it was built, the road remains an engineering marvel best appreciated at low speeds. Photo © Douglas Peebles. **Preceding spread:** A rare cloudless morning reveals the gulches, streams and rain forests of Haleakalā's majestic southeast flank. 'Ohe'o Gulch and its Seven Pools are visible at center. Once slated for resort development, the gem-like freshwater pools are now part of Haleakalā National Park. Photo © Shane Tegarden. **Following spread:** Developed from former ranch and pineapple lands, the Kapalua Resort includes a craggy coast, crescent beaches, verdant golf fairways, and dark pine windbreaks. Photo © Ron Dahlquist.

Left: A cloudless day reveals the cinder cone-studded interior of Haleakalā. Vast enough to swallow Manhattan, the summit is the legendary home of the sun and the one-time abode of the Hawaiian volcano goddess Pele. Varying cinder colors indicate successive eruptions. Photo © Douglas Peebles.

Following spread: Backed by homes, fairway estates and farmland, Maui's first "destination resort" forms a graceful curve along the sandy Kā'anapali shoreline. Photo © Douglas Peebles.

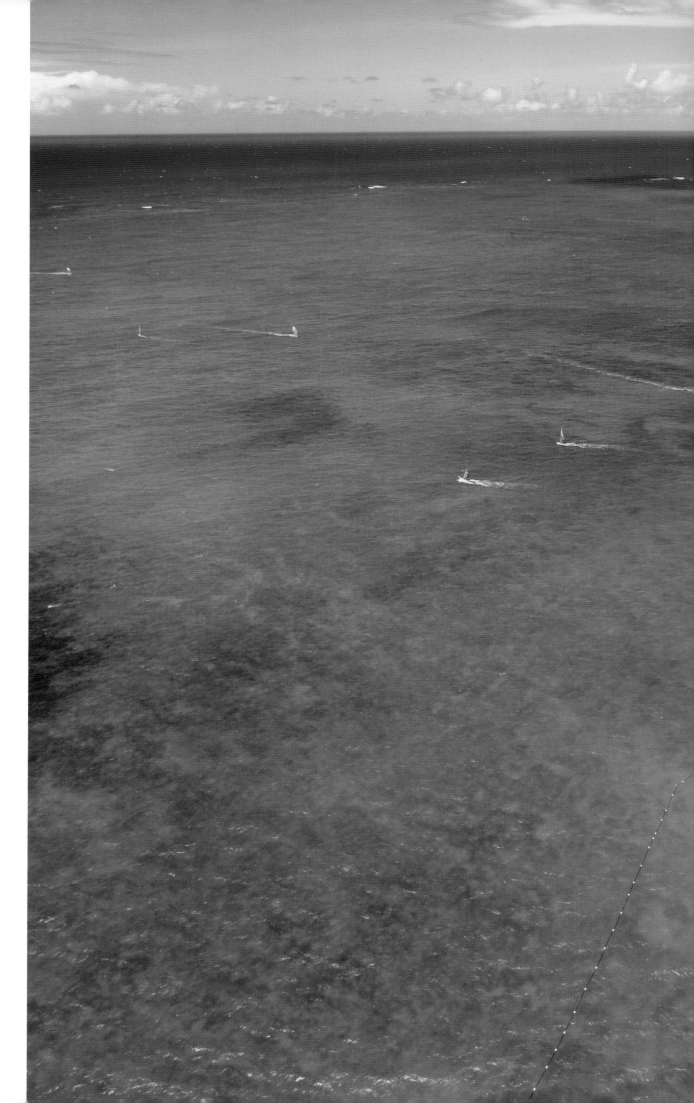

Right: Thread-like wakes trail windsurfers across the shallow, turquoise waters of Kanahā Beach Park. The Kahului Airport runway is visible at upper right. Photo © Douglas Peebles.

Following spread: Developed from former ranch land, the hotels and condominiums of the Wailea Resort share a string of sandy coves along Maui's sunny southern coast. Photo © Ron Dahlquist

Above: Like Maui's big toe, the Pu'u Ōla'i cinder cone probes the ocean off Mākena. Tucked up against Pu'u Ōla'i is Little Beach, a popular sunbathing and wave riding spot. Big Beach, or Oneloa, curves off to the right. Photo © Ron Dahlquist. **Opposite:** Condominiums, mini-malls and restaurants line busy South Kīhei Road, visible just inland from the Kama'ole beach parks. Kīhei is Maui's newest and fastest-growing community. Photo © Ron Dahlquist.

Left: After over a century spent at the epicenter of Maui's economic life, the sugar industry has ceded influence to the island's burgeoning tourism and real estate sectors. But as this view of the Hawaiian Commercial Sugar Company's Pu'unēnē factory suggests, HC&S remains a major employer, landowner and water distributor, producing sugar from 25,000 acres of Central Maui cane fields. Smart engineering, self-sufficient energy and centralized operations have enabled HC&S to stay in business long after Hawai'i's other sugar mills have closed down. Plantation days are not over yet, but plantation life— camps, camp housing, camp stores, plantation run public programs and facilities— which contributed so much to Maui's heritage are a thing of the past. Photo © Douglas Peebles.

Scenic Scapes

*O*nce upon a time, Maui was four islands large. Maui and its three closest neighbors—Kaho'olawe, Lāna'i and Moloka'i—once formed a single land mass. In effect, Maui was the "big island" before the Big Island came along.

As all Hawaiian Islands do, this mega-Maui eventually settled back into the ocean, like a giant easing down into a bathtub.

Mega-Maui's five volcanoes remained above water, as did their upland slopes and saddles. But the lowlands linking those five mountains sank into the deep. In a blink of geologic time, one island became four smaller ones, interlaced by ocean channels.

So Maui had to surrender the title of "biggest island." But it wasn't a total loss. In exchange, the four new islands all got wraparound ocean views. Some views had other islands off in the distance.

Scenery-wise, it was a good tradeoff.

As the highest of the four islands, Maui got the best deal.

From its 10,000-foot summit on a clear day, a panorama view takes in Hawai'i, Kaho'olawe, Lāna'i and Moloka'i. And once in a blue moon, just after dawn, you can even see O'ahu.

The proximity to other islands, many channels, and the various weather gives Maui scenic backdrops to die for. Add channel squalls, wind-blown rainbows, yachts under sail, and humpbacks blowing and breaching, and the offshore scenery becomes sublime.

But as the following pages attest, one needn't only look offshore for scenery. Because Maui kept the two biggest volcanoes for itself, the island has sublime mountain scenery as well.

Soaring above 10,000 feet, Haleakalā has features normally associated with continents—alpine flora and fauna, "alpenglow" light effects, a tree line and even, every so often, a snow line. The mountain's vast eroded caldera trumps all that with multi-colored cinder cones, craggly cliffs and canyons, flocks of geese in flight, and its own rain forest.

Maui's other volcano, variously called West Maui or Pu'u Kukui, rises only a mile high, but cedes no scenic ground. As the elder mountain, Pu'u Kukui has had much longer to erode. Its cliffs are day-glo green, incredibly steep and mystically cloud-hung. Its slopes are riven with waterfalls and mantled in jungle greenery. As one of earth's wettest places, the ancient Pu'u Kukui caldera is a wonderland of streams, hidden pools, fallen fruit and fragrant forests.

Of course, each volcano also has exterior slopes, and a scenery that never stops. It also varies dramatically. In a half-hour on West Maui, a scenery-hungry motorist could ascend from the beach, through the desert, past cane fields and high meadows and into deep jungle. Haleakalā is twice as big, so the same plan might take an hour.

Traveling laterally opens up even more scenery. A single Maui circuit would take you around two mountains, across two deserts, through two rain forests, over a hundred stream beds, and past countless cliffs, beaches, pools, forests, waterfalls, gorges, ravines, ridges, hills, pastures and valleys.

Oh, and a tunnel.

"Garanz-ballbaranz," as Mauians used to say, there's a photo op in there somewhere.

Above: Interlaced coral trees form a fragrant corridor of bright blossoms over this sparsely traveled road in Kīpahulu on Maui's Hāna Coast. Photo © Douglas Peebles. **Opposite:** Seen from West Maui's Nāpili Bay on a windless evening, a fiery sunset silhouettes coconut palms and the distant island of Lāna'i. Photo © Douglas Peebles. **Preceding spread:** Sunset and a long exposure transform a late summer south swell into a Maui creation story of earth, sea and sky. Photo © Quincy Dean.

Right: An East Maui dawn paints soft sky pastels over Ke'anae, a leaf-shaped peninsula formed by lava flows from Haleakalā. The craggy headland is home to several families of Hawaiian taro farmers, two historic churches, and a picturesque ball park. Photo © Shane Tegarden.

Preceding spread: The older of Maui's two volcanoes, Pu'u Kukui's jungled slopes, mile-high cliffs and knife-edge ridges attest to eons of erosion. Very few hikers have ever summited the peak at right, which looks accessible but is subject to sudden and severe weather changes. Photo © Tony Novak-Clifford.

Near Nāhiku, twin waterfalls tumble out of mixed forest and over a precipice of eroded lava. The trees visible in the foreground include stately Norfolk Island pines, cliff-hugging hala trees, and scattered coconut palms. The mystery: how did they get to this lofty Eden? Photo © Bob Bangerter.

Right: Jacaranda trees form a fragrant purple cloud over these ranch houses on Haleakalā's Upcountry slopes. The trees bloom for several weeks each spring. Photo © Cindy Campbell.

Preceding spread: Morning light enobles the sapphire waters, verdant cliffs and palm-fringed black sand cove at Wai'ānapanapa on the Hāna Coast. Photo © Rob DeCamp.

Above: This star-streaked time exposure reveals why Haleakalā has been a celestial vantage point for centuries, first for Hawaiians, and now for astronomers. Photo © Rob DeCamp. **Opposite:** A rare silversword plant brightens the mountain's scenic but arid terrain. Photo © Scott Mead.

Right: Late afternoon sun highlights a taro pond and the manicured grounds of a Keʻanae homestead. In Hawaiian legend, the taro plant was the first being created by the gods and a sibling to humans. The leaves and starchy corms are a dietary staple across Polynesia. Photo © Shane Tegarden.

Preceding spread: Also called "cloud country," Haleakalā's broad leeward flank is home to many equestrian stables like this handsome complex near Makawao. Late 19th century settlers from the Madeira and Azores Islands made Upcountry towns like Makawao, Haʻikū and Kula a robust Portuguese enclave. Photo © Douglas Peebles.

Left: Some parts of Maui feel like Southeast Asia, particularly the bamboo forests of Kailua and Kīpahulu. Photo © David Schoonover.

Following spread, left: Late afternoon waves splash a lava outcrop at Kīhei's Poʻolenalena Beach. Visible in the middle distance is Mākena's Puʻu Ōlaʻi cinder cone. Photo © Michael and Monica Sweet.

Following spread, right: A breathless sunset and a skillful time exposure create a tropical tableau, which is visible from a wave swept Mākena cove. Lānaʻi Island rises in the middle distance. Photo © Rob DeCamp.

Right: The neon-green winter grass at this Upcountry ranch contrasts strikingly with the sere and gullied volcanic slopes in the distance. Maui's high country forage has nourished free-range beef cattle for over a century. Photo © David Olsen.

Preceding spread: Mākena's peerless Oneloa (long sand) beach forms a mile-long crescent along Haleakalā's sunny southern shore. The steep sand bank at water's edge hints the ocean is not always this tranquil. Photo © David Olsen.

Following spread: Three of the Big Island's five volcanoes are visible over Haleakalā's eroded southern rim. From left are Mauna Kea, Mauna Loa and Hualālai. According to legend, the cinder cone at center right is where the volcano goddess Pele planted her 'ō'ō digging stick when she vaulted to a new home on the Big Island. Photo © Frank J. Wicker.

Coconut palms rustle in the late afternoon breeze along Mākena's Maluaka Beach. The cloud-capped "island" in the middle distance is actually West Maui. Photo © Douglas Peebles.

Conservation

Gaze out over Maui.

If you're like most people, you'll see natural beauty so striking you might call this place paradise, as millions of others have.

Your senses would bear that out. The weather is blissfully warm and mild. The beaches are golden, the ocean a sparkling prism of sapphire and turquoise. The volcanic slopes are a checkerboard of farms, forests and pastures.

No doubt about it: this island is stunningly beautiful. That's the story most often told, and the one most people want to hear.

But there's another story: Maui is also vulnerable. Its beauty is not bulletproof. Its resources are not limitless. If the island is to continue to thrive in the future, it will need conservation.

That story has so far been a mixed one.

In ancient times, the Hawaiians developed systems of farming, fishing and resource allocation so sophisticated they sustained a million people on eight small islands. But the same systems also doomed many species of insects, plants and birds unique in the world.

Hawaiians suffered a holocaust when outsiders introduced terrible new diseases and an exploitative economic system. Within 50 years of Captain Cook's arrival in 1778, Hawai'i had lost a thousand-year-old culture, most of its people, and all of its sandalwood.

Over the next century, very little was conserved. What could be sold was sold; what could be profitably used was used; what could not be used was replaced. Forests were cut down. Streams were dammed and diverted. Grasslands were overgrazed. Top soil blew away or sluiced into the sea. The loss of unique species accelerated.

Statehood in 1959 brought new challenges as policymakers reconfigured the islands as a vacation Mecca for millions. Seemingly overnight, towns become cities, reefs become runways, marshes became suburbs, and beaches were scooped up for concrete.

Maui was spared much of this. The island was the territory of a few large and relatively conservative landowners, rather than thousands of small ones. These deep-pocketed plantations and ranches could develop carefully planned communities and destination resorts rather than selling off their lands piecemeal.

Maui also has benefited over the years from the work of citizen conservationists. In the early 1970s, a handful of influential Kīpahulu transplants, led by airline executive Sam Pryor, plied their financial and publishing connections to save Seven Pools from resort development. The natural gem was instead deeded to Haleakalā National Park.

A decade later, the small but fiercely committed Maui citizens' group SPAM defeated a proposal to build 10 hotels at Mākena, thus conserving Maui's most popular beach for future generations. Shortly thereafter, a Hawaiian coalition prevailed upon Kapalua developers to re-site a major hotel away from nearby ancient burials.

Since then, conservation has gradually gained traction on Maui. Citizens' groups now promote reef health, upland reforestation, protection of threatened species, control of dangerous new ones, and restoration of streams and watersheds. Institutions like the Coastal Land Trust and the Sierra Club work to "land bank" and preserve ecologically sensitive acreage.

The result is the Maui you see today. If you cherish what you see, you must as the Hawaiians say, "Malama 'āina," take care of this place.

Above: Preservationist Randy Bartlett cradles the blossoms of a rare Maui lobelia, a species that dates back to prehistoric times. Photo © David Watersun. **Opposite:** Cloaked in mist, slicker-clad conservationists observe a flowering lobelia that survives in a marshy "lost world" atop West Maui's mile-high Pu'u Kukui volcano. The site's inaccessibility has preserved species that have vanished elsewhere in Hawai'i. Photo © Ron Dahlquist. **Preceding spread:** As two boys look on, Walter Pū (in water), Ben Villiarimo and Hank Eharis inventory a boulder-strewn Hāna Coast shoreline for edible limpets called 'opihi. The Nature Conservancy 'Opihi Partnership seeks to restore the popular shellfish, which are so over-harvested on Maui they are now imported from Ireland. Photo © Bob Bangerter.

Above: So rare and fragile is the wetland atop Puʻu Kukui, that volunteers need medical clearances to qualify for a lottery for helicopter seats. Once at the top, they must cross the marsh on raised walkways. Photo © Ron Dahlquist. **Opposite:** Maui Conservationist Art Medeiros helps a volunteer plant a native koa seedling in the Auwahi cloud forest on the heavily eroded back side of Haleakalā. The group seeks to restore an ancient watershed destroyed by deforestation and overgrazing. Photo © Ron Dahlquist.

Above: This bright red 'i'iwi is among the few survivors of Maui's once-abundant native forest bird population. Its distinctive curved bill enables the 'i'iwi to feed on flower nectar. Large upland areas of Maui are set aside as preserves for endangered bird species. Photo © Anita Harris. **Opposite:** An endangered forest bird, the Maui 'amakihi eyes faces danger in the form of a honeybee working the same cluster of flowers. Rodents and insects imported to Maui by humans have driven many of the native birds to the brink of extinction. Photo © Bob Bangerter. **Preceding spread, left:** Harnessing sustainable energy sources to go off the grid is a goal of forward-looking East Maui residents. This Ha'ikū homestead built by Eric Bryant features a windmill, a power shed and photovoltaic panels. Photo © Darrell Wong. **Preceding spread, right:** Hikers explore the rain forest ecology of East Maui's Ke'anae Arboretum, situated along the Hāna Coast road. Like most of Maui, the arboretum is a patchwork of native and invasive species. Photo © Douglas Peebles.

Left: Predation, disease and habitat loss caused a collapse of the Hawaiian monk seal population, from which the species has not recovered. Occasionally seen hauled out to rest on Maui beaches, these gravely endangered marine mammals are federally protected today. Photo © Bob Bangerter.

Preceding spread: A mother-calf humpback whale pair cruise the warm, limpid waters of Maui's shallow channels. Once hunted to near extinction, the North Pacific humpback population that migrates between Alaska and Hawai'i is now federally protected and steadily recovering. Photo © David Olsen.

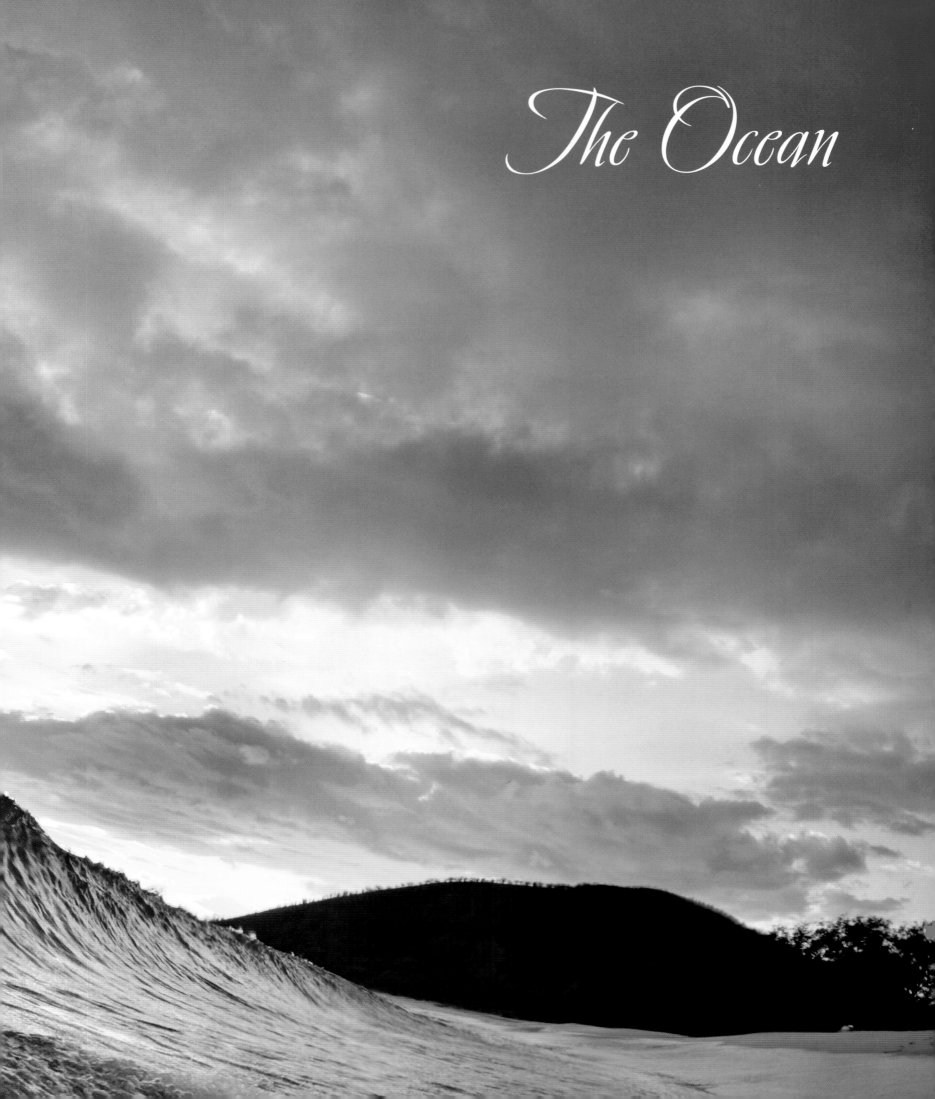

The Ocean

aui tour drivers have to keep a straight face when fielding the question posed to them: "Does the ocean go all the way around the island?"

Yes, Virginia, it does. It goes waaaaay around the island.

Oddly, it's not such a weird question. Nearly everyone who reaches Maui these days does so by air. Most shut their view ports soon after takeoff, bend over laptops, magazines and video games, and await meal service and the movie.

Preferring not to think about the life vests under the seats, they insert ear buds, recline chair backs, fluff blankets and ride across the Pacific in comfy denial.

A few open their window shades for the approach to Kahului, but by then the "ocean" part is over. Their memory of crossing it is a half-day blank. And when the plane rolls to a stop, presto! It's all land again. Let's go do something.

Things were different when everyone used to arrive by sea. Back then, instead of land-air-land, the trip was more like: land-ocean-ocean-ocean-ocean-more ocean-days more ocean-and finally, LAAAAAAAND!

To those voyagers, Maui or any other island requiring such a daunting passage would have seemed miraculous. Instead of driving blithely off to buy donuts, they would have kissed the ground in a rapture of gratitude and deliverance.

For Maui is miraculous. Like its Hawaiian neighbors and the other far-flung islands of Polynesia, Micronesia and Melanesia, it's just a pinhead in the Pacific. When seen from space these islands barely exist at all. We should appreciate them much more than we do.

What's more, Maui is not simply *in* the ocean. It is of the ocean. Its name honors the god who fished Polynesia from the sea floor. Maui arose from there as well. Layer by layer, over geologic ages, Maui built itself up out of stygian darkness toward daylight.

Now we land-dwellers enjoy a blink of time before Maui erodes back into the ocean again. From a geologic perspective, our experience here would be: ocean-blink-ocean. The island part is the anomaly.

The Hawaiians understood this. An elderly Hawaiian once counseled a malihini (visitor) who was skipping stones from a Maui beach. "The ocean is our mother," he said, not unkindly. "Do you throw stones at your mother?"

The mother ocean that gives life to Maui is alive. Its primal waters sustain a universe of forces and currents, of plants and creatures great and small. The ancient chant "kumulipo" voices the Hawaiian idea that everything dwelling on land has a double in the sea, and the pairs are spiritually entwined. As above, so is below.

The kumulipo also suggests that island, ocean and sky—and all therein— are one living system. We tend to ignore that now, amid our modern distractions, just as we ignore the life vests beneath the seats.

Maui might be better served if we land-dwellers went into the ocean more often. After all, that's not just big blue scenery out there. It's our life.

Above: A female green sea turtle glides through clear Maui waters. Once hunted for their shells and meat, the big turtles are now protected and are slowly recovering. Some females come ashore on Maui beaches to lay their eggs. Photo © Michael and Monica Sweet. **Opposite:** Scuba divers ready underwater lights to explore one of the cathedral cave formations off Maui's neighbor island, Lānai. Water clarity at some popular dive sites allows visibility approaching 200 feet. Photo © David Fleetham. **Preceding spread:** Sunset backlights skim boarder Kegan Conway riding the shore break at Mākena's Oneloa Beach. A hybrid of surfing and skateboarding, skimming has found a home on Maui shores. Coarse sand and steep inclines allow riders to skim down wet sand, then turn and ride incoming waves back up the beach. Photo © Quincy Dean.

Left: The newest addition to the Maui water sports inventory is kite boarding, as shown here at Kanahā Beach Park near the Kahului Airport. Riders like this one use wing-like kites and short, double-ended boards for high speed aerial acrobatics. Kite boarders share the windy Kanahā shoreline with surfers, canoe teams, divers and windsurfers. Photo © Quincy Dean.

Preceding spread: A stoked boogie boarder Forrest Dein gets shacked in a pitching Mākena tube. Mākena's Oneloa Beach is a favorite with Maui belly boarders, as are Baldwin Park and Pā'ia Bay on the island's windward side. The old Hawaiian version of the sport employed flat wooden wave skimmers called paipo boards. Photo © Quincy Dean.

Following spread: Called OC-1s, these nimble one-person outrigger canoes first became popular as off-season trainers for regular six-person canoe paddling. But as this ocean race photo suggests, the smaller, lighter boats have definitely come into their own. Here dozens of racers enjoy the fast, downwind run from Maliko to Kahului. Photo © Darrell Wong.

Right: Once Maui's long best-kept secret, the monster waves at Pe'ahi's remote Jaws surf break gained global notoriety after National Geographic featured it in a cover story. The shape and configuration of the deep, stream-fed bay and its undersea pinnacles supersizes incoming north swells to freakish proportions. The largest waves are so big they cannot be paddled into. Riders must use sail power or jet skis. Here tow-in surfer Laird Hamilton drops in way back on one of the largest waves ever ridden on Maui. Photo © Bob Bangerter.

Above: On Maui, you're never too young to get into the waves. Here champion skim boarder Nohea Bachiller busts a tricky aerial move in choppy shore break. Skim boards are amphibious—they fly across wet sand or wave faces with equal dexterity. Photo © Bob Bangerter. **Opposite:** Champion windsurfer and big wave rider Robby Naish shows how boardsailing skill enabled early windsurfers to challenge the fearsome North Maui break Jaws. Naish spent years on Maui pioneering board, sail and equipment designs that revolutionized windsurfing world-wide. Photo © Darrell Wong. **Following spread:** A men's team from Maui's Kīhei Canoe Club blasts up and over a foaming whitecap during the annual Moloka'i Ho'e channel race. First paddled in 1952, the race sends paddlers churning 40 miles across the Ka'iwi Channel from Moloka'i to O'ahu each fall. Held on separate weekends, the men's and women's races each draw dozens of crews from all over Hawai'i and the Pacific. Photo © Shane Tegarden.

Left: Scuba divers eye raccoon butterfly fish schooling over a shallow Maui reef. Maui's clear water and numerous "put-in" spots make much of the island accessible to shore-based snorkelers and divers. Half-day boats and interisland charters serve those seeking deeper dives and remoter sites. Photo © David Fleetham.

Above: As if replicating the fluke pattern on the valley walls behind it, a sounding humpback whale plunges toward deep water off Olowalu. The whales seen off Maui are part of a North Pacific humpback population that migrates between Alaska and Hawai'i. Once reduced to a few hundred, this community now numbers in the low thousands, thanks to federal protection. Photo © Michael and Monica Sweet. **Opposite:** Few Maui sights are more dramatic than seeing a 40-ton humpback whale breach in open water. The splash from a good breach can be seen for miles. Visible behind this arching giant are the slopes behind Lahaina. Photo © Michael and Monica Sweet. **Preceding spread:** Often sighted off Maui and Lāna'i, spinner dolphins are among the marine mammal world's top acrobats. In addition to leaping effortlessly from the water, they also flip, twirl and spin like Olympic springboard divers. This playful spinner pod plunges into a well-synchronized splashdown. Photo © David Fleetham.

Left: A lone surfer makes a lissome silhouette against this south Maui sunset. While not as notorious as Jaws and other north shore breaks, the island's south side boasts numerous wave riding spots, especially during the summer months. Photo © Michael and Monica Sweet.

Preceding spread: Displaying its distinctive scars, ventral striations and hitch-hiking barnacles, a humpback whale swims just beneath the ocean surface off Maui. Individual whales can be identified from the patterning and coloration of their fins and flukes. Photo © David Olsen.

Nature Maui

A Kīhei resident wheeling in the trash cans glances over his shoulder to see a humpback whale breaching in bright water offshore. A glance over the other shoulder catches a ghostly mantle of fog sifting through redwoods on the mountainside.

A woman in Kula looks up from her kitchen sink to see an owl hovering at her window, gazing in at her. Visitors on a Kāʻanapali hotel terrace startle to the "chk chk chk" of gecko lizards on the window screen.

Hāliʻimaile kids riding bikes to the basketball court see rain falling on one side of the road, but not on the other. They weave in and out of the soft wet curtain.

Moments like these occur continuously on Maui. Only about 10 percent of the island is urbanized; encounters with the natural world are so commonplace as to seem, well, natural. And, unusual exceptions aside, Maui's nature is a benign and welcoming one.

The climate is tropical; weather is generally warm, breezy and mild. In most parts of the island, there's so little temperature change between inside and outside that islanders use their carports as family rooms. School children rarely lose boots, scarves or jackets, because they don't need or have them.

The same gentle conditions bless the natural world. Vegetation sprouts like crazy in Maui's rich volcanic soils. Trees shoot skyward like Jack's beanstalk. Ferns carpet the forest floor. Fruits and flowers perfume the air. Grasses green the meadows. The water in Maui's streams falls right out of the sky, clear, clean and cool.

Down along the shore, the sands are soft and inviting, the waves warm and blue. Minnows dart through tide pools. Ghost crabs scurry across damp sand. Seaweeds dance a lissome hula in the shallows. Just beyond lies the busy crackle of the reef; fish, shrimp, urchins and eels move among bright corals. Further out, turtles, rays, sharks, dolphins, pelagic fishes, and whales cruise the waters.

Whole ranges of other species live on Maui's deserts and arid leeward slopes—thorny cactuses and kiawe trees, hummocks of elephant grass, coveys of quail, chukars and pheasants, nēnē geese and white-tailed deer. The scenery changes on the other side of the rain line. Now it is guava and wild plum, jungle vines and wild pigs, neon chameleons and whining drifts of mosquitoes.

It is amazing that so much nature thrives on one small island, but its accessibility is no less remarkable. In many other places, people travel for hours or days to experience such variety. On Maui, we just step outside and look around.

This Eden-like quality can be misleading. As discussed elsewhere in this book, Maui's natural balance is a fragile one. Species introduced carelessly to this tropical ecosystem can wreak havoc very swiftly. Likewise, short-sighted land use and ocean-use policies can have disastrous consequences to the island's natural resources.

Fortunately, Maui's natural bounty is now increasingly recognized and valued by isle policymakers, residents and visitors. Safeguarding that precious resource is only natural.

Above: One of Maui's most popular nursery and landscaping tropicals is the vivid heliconia. Its tall stalks and hanging flower clusters are ideal for showy arrangements. Photo © Michael and Monica Sweet. **Opposite:** Also called pin cushions, these wiry sunburst protea blooms grow especially well in Kula. They are hardy enough to pack and ship, and their unorthodoxy appeals to flower arrangers. Photo © Douglas Peebles. **Preceding spread:** Red leaf and green leaf ti plants mix with other colorful tropicals in a typical East Maui landscape display. The district's abundant rainfall, volcanic soil and warm weather encourage robust plant growth, whether desired or not. Photo © Laurent Martres.

Backlit by a rising sun and pink-tinted clouds, a stand of blooming silversword plants greets hikers along a Haleakalā trail. The rare plants grow at ground level for years, then send up a thick column of sticky red flowers. Photo © Ron Dahlquist.

A handsome chukar commands an enviable vantage overlooking Haleakalā.
Chukar, quail and pheasants are among game birds popular with Maui hunters.
Photo © Anita Harris.

Right: Mosses, Bird's-nest ferns, tree-hugging vines, ti plants and guava trees form the understory for this lush Maui rain forest. The taller trunks of palms and kukui trees stretch toward sunlight filtering through the dense canopy above. Some regions of Maui are among the world's rainiest places. Photo © Quincy Dean.

Following spread, left: Its beak curved to draw nectar from particular plants, this juvenile 'i'iwi bird sips sustenance from *lobelia grayana* blossoms. The survival of Hawai'i's remaining native birds depends upon conservation of upland watersheds and protection of remote cloud forest habitats. Photo © Michael R. Neal.

Following spread, right: The black-crowned night heron is a relatively recent arrival on Maui. This one has found a stone perch near a stream bank. Like other herons, this one is a shallow water feeder, with a long beak designed for piercing. Photo © Ron Dahlquist.

Above: Juicy mountain apples ripen at the Maui Nui Botanical Gardens in Kahului. Maui is too tropical for conventional apples, but these soft, sweet, apple-like fruits thrive in local forests. Open to the public, the botanical garden fosters native plants and unusual imports. Photo © Douglas Peebles. **Opposite:** This purple spray is one of the prize blooms of the Maui Orchid Society, a group of dedicated growers who stage orchid shows and trade cultivation tips. Many Maui patios and backyards house orchid greenhouses. Photo © Douglas Peebles. **Preceding spread, left:** Its grooved footpads enable this blue-green gecko to cling to the undersides of leaves, scale trees, scamper up windows and even cross ceilings. This one has found a temporary home on a banana leaf. Photo © Cameron Nelson. **Preceding spread, right:** With its rolling eye pouches, ridged skin and triplicate horn, this Jackson chameleon resembles a saurian from some bygone age. Like many invasive or imported species, these taciturn, slow-moving tree dwellers have found an ecological niche on Maui. Photo © David Watersun.

Right: Thought to have evolved from Canada geese blown off-course long ago, these rare Hawaiian nēnē geese dwell in Haleakalā and at a few other sites on Maui, Molokaʻi and the Big Island. The present colony of 200-300 geese is protected by the state government, which declared the nēnē Hawaiʻi's state bird. Photo © Frank J. Wicker.

Preceding spread: Native to India and Southeast Asia, banyan trees like this big pīpīwai banyan at Kīpahulu long ago muscled their way into Hawaiʻi's ecosystem. As they grow, some banyans drop aerial roots that become new trunks, enabling the trees to claim ever wider territorial spheres. One famous Lahaina banyan occupies a city block and is more than a century old. Photo © Laurent Martres.

Following spread, left: The aptly-named happy face spider is among rare native insects that evolved to fill particular ecological niches in Hawaiʻi. Along with some native birds, some Hawaiian insect species have perished due to habitat loss and competition from invaders. On the other hand, some well-hidden native species are only now being discovered. Photo © Bob Bangerter.

Following spread, right: A staple of the Polynesian diet, breadfruit like these specimens at the Maui Nui Botanical Gardens are rich in carbohydrates and are usually eaten baked. Breadfruit trees have broad, showy leaves, massive trunks and branches, and a rapid growth trajectory, as some backyard arborists learn to their dismay. Photo © Douglas Peebles.

Hawaiian Ways

Maui is one of the Hawaiian Islands, but it is also a "Hawaiian" island. Directly or indirectly, Hawaiian values and Hawaiian ways shape every Maui moment.

Like many other aspects of the island experience, that's easier said than understood. A popular bumper sticker encourages people to "Respect the Culture." But what exactly is the culture?

Is it aloha, or pit bulls? Facial tattoos, or slack-key guitar? Dancing hula, or spearing ulua? None of the above, or all the above?

The visitor industry calls the Hawaiians the state's *host culture,* a term that can be taken several ways. One implication is that Hawaiians should be accorded the respect rightfully due a host. But another reading implies Hawaiians should feel a "host-guest" responsibility for non-Hawaiians. That replays some troubling old tapes.

In the decades after a cabal of American businessmen overthrew Hawai'i's monarchy, Hollywood and Tin Pan Alley popularized a prototypical "Hawaiian" who was, among other things, easy-going, musical, funny, friendly, lazy, addled and goofy.

History suggests a different image. During the monarchy period, the Hawaiians, from whom present-day islanders descend, were the most literate and learned people in the Pacific. And before being decimated by foreign diseases, their forebearers had been extraordinary warriors. Along with keen intelligence, the early warrior culture valued rigorous conditioning, aggressiveness, courage, cunning, skill in battle, and above all, the ability to withstand pain without complaint.

These are bedrock Hawaiian values, and they infuse many aspects of modern Maui life. In the physical realm alone, relentless

conditioning and a fierce will to win inform pursuits as varied as hula dancing, martial arts, ball sports, board sailing, rodeo and canoe racing, all of which in Maui excels.

Courage, skill and endurance are equally venerated. A typical Hawaiian rite of passage challenges youths to slay a wild boar and land a hundred-pound ulua within the same year. Endurance of pain is institutionalized in the expression "can handle" and in the smiling acceptance of hula's torturous training regimes.

To sustain armies in the field, the ancient Hawaiians had to master many callings. Maui's farmers, hunters and fishers ranked among Polynesia's most prolific providers. Island cloth makers, weavers, carvers, astronomers, healers, feather workers and canoe builders brought to their arts the same depth of devotion.

Although skill sets have changed, aptitudes and attitudes remain the same. The spirit of lōkahi (shared commitment) and kōkua (mutual helpfulness) that once guided the ancestors is still alive wherever modern Mauians gather, be it for a family construction project or for an island-wide charity walk.

The Hawaiian precepts of pono (what a Buddhist might term right action) and 'ohana (a caring, extended family) also enrich island life today. Put simply, the Maui 'ohana embraces those who respectfully adhere to the precepts of kōkua, lōkahi and pono. Hawaiian blood may not be essential, but Hawaiian heart is.

Finally, Mauians are rightfully proud of their island. The Hawaiian saying "Maui no ka 'oi" (Maui is the best) is by now familiar to millions.

True Mauians live it.

Above: Garlanded in greenery, a young dancer honors with her devotion, suppleness and grace the ancient Hawaiian art of hula. Her garlands are multiple strands of yellow-green Pakalana blossoms, highly prized for lei making. Her haku or head lei is woven from hand-picked mountain and forest plants. Photo © Shane Tegarden. **Opposite:** Cloaked in a rustling, rain-repellent cape of dry leaves, a spear-bearing lua (martial arts) warrior guards an assembly of high chiefs at Mākena. Photo © Shane Tegarden. **Preceding spread:** Symbolically uniting the island, outrigger and sailing canoes represent the various moku or districts of Maui as they come ashore at Wailea Beach. Ceremonial greeter Kimokea Kapahulehua welcomes the morning arrivals to a Maui Native Hawaiian Chamber of Commerce gathering at the Grand Wailea Hotel. Photo © Shane Tegarden.

Above: Maui videographer and mahi ʻai (farmer) Calvin Kuamoʻo checks the leaves of mature kalo (taro) plants. Both the kalo leaves and corms are staples in the traditional Hawaiian diet. The corms can be steamed and pounded into poi. Photo © Shane Tegarden. **Opposite:** The tiered black lava stonework of Hāna's famous Piʻilani Heiau (temple) backdrops this patch of taro growing in Kahanu Gardens. Different varieties of taro can be cultivated in shallow ponds or in dry lands terraces. Photo © Douglas Peebles.

Right: With help from her granddaughter Rose Pi'ilani Bailey, dance teacher Gordean Bailey chants with her hālau Wehiwehi O Leilehua Hula Pā during a ceremony at Kahikinui ("the greater Tahiti") on Haleakalā's arid southeast slopes. Fragrant maile strands and other vines associated with the hula goddess Laka circle the chanters, their drums and their gourds. Photo © Shane Tegarden.

Preceding spread: Sam Kaha'i Ka'ai pours 'awa for cup bearer Lokewa Lono who will serve an honored guest, (not shown) and Kamana'o Crabbe (third from left). Ke'eaumoku Kapu (far left) and Kamana'o Crabbe (third from left) are assisting Sam Ka'ai in the 'awa protocol. Photo © Shane Tegarden.

Following spread, left: The late Charles Ka'upu, a prominent hula teacher, chanter and mentor, had promoted Hawaiian culture in many ways, including coaching island high school students and joining studio musicians in genre-bending recording projects. His voice is unmistakable. Photo © Randy Jay Braun.

Following spread, right: The bearer of an illustrious island name, Sam Kalalau III is both a Hawaiian cultural mentor and a modern policymaker. Son of the late trans-Polynesian voyaging canoe crewman Sam Kalalau Jr., Sam III has served on a commission to reclaim and reforest the former Navy target island of Kaho'olawe. Photo © Shane Tegarden.

Left: Running a large modern hālau, or hula school, is a daunting venture requiring a serious commitment from everyone. Here Maui kumu hula Uluwehi Guerrero presents his entire Hālau Hula Kauluokalā on the stage of the Maui Arts and Cultural Center. Photo © Shane Tegarden.

Preceding spread: Like the legendary demigod Maui was named for, Daniel Wallace seems to cast his throw net over the sun. If his aim is true, this Olowalu fisherman could feed the family with one throw. Photo © David Olsen.

Following spread: Fern-garlanded dancers from the hula school Hālau Ke'alaokamaile perform in the kahiko (traditional) division of the Haku Mele chant, chorus and dance competition in Hāna. Photo © Shane Tegarden.

Right: Brandishing pipipi bracelets and necklaces fashioned from fresh-water shellfish, dancers perform at the Haku Mele contest in Hāna. An important part of hālau training is learning to collect, create and wear one's own costumes and ornaments. Prayers, protocols and intense preparation precede any serious hula endeavor. Photo © Shane Tegarden.

Following spread, left: Blowing a conch shell, pū, to awaken the dawn, Hawaiian practitioner Kimokea Kapahulehua sends a clarion call to canoes waiting beneath a rainbow just offshore. Photo © Shane Tegarden.

Following spread, right: Many island drums are hollowed out of coconut palm trunks, but this unusual instrument was carved from kukui wood. Also called candle nut trees, mature kukui trees shower the ground with hard, oily seeds that in olden days were pierced and strung together to form time-release candles. Photo © David Watersun.

Maui Life

On Maui, "lifestyle" is a simple word but a complex reality.

Because the island is home to many ethnic groups, nationalities and economic strata, there are actually quite a few Maui lifestyles.

Some Mauians travel in private jets, reside in gated mansions, and employ their own chefs and fitness trainers. Other Mauians get around on foot, eat at church soup kitchens, and sleep on the beach. It's a wide range, one that is just economically diverse. Stir in nationality, ethnicity, religion, culture, language and lineage, and you're talking about dozens of Maui lifestyles. 'Uku plenny, in pidgin.

All these lifestyles coexist, but they don't all coincide. Put another way, Maui is more a stew than a soup.

There are some common ingredients, though.

The essential one is respect. If the various Maui lifestyles have a common denominator, it is respect for other people's values, attitudes and situations. This comes down from plantation times, when people from many cultures lived together in camps and learned to get along. Mauians may not agree on everything, but they agree to respect their differences.

This leads to a second vital seasoning for the Maui stew: consideration. To live harmoniously on an island, you need to consider other people's feelings and behave accordingly. For most islanders, this is as automatic as removing one's slippers at the doorstep or restraining from honking the car horn in traffic. Why be rude?

A sense of humor is another island essential. Mauians enjoy many styles and forms of humor, so laughter is as ever-present as

the wind. In the plantation days, workers imported from distant parts of the world did not always understand each other, but they always found ways to laugh together. That legacy endures today. Equally important is the ability to laugh at one's self, and to tease and be teased.

Except where infirmity precludes it, outdoor activity is another Maui lifestyle ingredient. From elders taking sunrise walks through Wailuku to daredevils skateboarding down Haleakalā by moonlight, Mauians love to go outside. For some, outside is an orchid greenhouse in the backyard. For others, it is the face of a 60-foot wave at Jaws. The difference is only of degree.

The Maui stew could not be as savory as it is without another key ingredient: enjoyment of other cultures. Most islanders treasure the diversity of customs, tastes and traditions that first the Hawaiians, then successive waves of in-migrants, brought with them. It's not unusual to see on a Maui menu favorites from Hawai'i, Sāmoa, Tonga, Okinawa, the Philippines, Thailand, Vietnam, China, Puerto Rico, Portugal, Mexico, Guatemala, Europe and the mainland. And those are just the appetizers.

Finally, Mauians share an appreciation for informality, friendliness and helpfulness. Despite the up-tempo growth of recent decades, the island remains a largely rural, small-town place. People still look after each other, work willingly together, leave mangoes on a neighbor's doorstep, stop anywhere to talk and laugh. It's guaranteed.

If you had to compress all of this into one word, it be *warm*. Maui is a warm place. It warms its people, and they warm each other.

Above: A pickup truck, a guitarist, and a smoldering Honolua sunset seem like a tableau for an ad campaign. But this is daily life on Maui. Photo © David Watersun. **Opposite:** Now in Wailuku, Sam Sato's restaurant has changed venues over the decades. But some things remain the same: portion size and loving presentation. Photo © Douglas Peebles. **Preceding spread:** Ivan Tam enjoys a longtime island tradition: the pancake breakfast at Wailuku's landmark Tasty Crust restaurant. It's a Maui essential. Photo © Douglas Peebles.

Above: A Maui landmark since 1927, Wailuku's handsomely restored 'Iao Theater continues to stage plays, films, concerts and political debates. Photo © Douglas Peebles. **Opposite:** A well-balanced stilt walker entertains a First Friday crowd in Wailuku. Every month, Maui's capitol blockades its main street for a party. Photo © Douglas Peebles. **Preceding spread, left:** Family members and friends pose proudly behind their handiwork in the Filipino food booth at a First Friday block party in Wailuku Town. Photo © Douglas Peebles. **Preceding spread, right:** The raffish north shore surf town of Pā'ia bestrides East Maui's rain line. Rainbows, sunshine and wet pavement coexist casually. Photo © Ron Dahlquist.

156

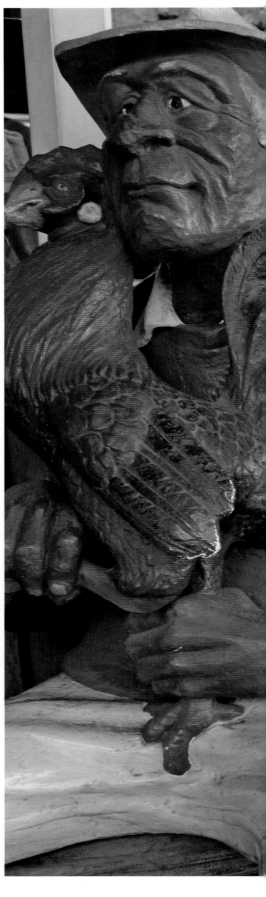

Above: Duke Kahanamoku's face peers from painted window louvers in the Ka'ahumanu Church rectory hall. The Wailuku church is among Maui's oldest. Photo © Terrie Eliker. **Opposite:** Sculpted by the late Reems Mitchell, life-size statues of Upcountry old timers amuse two members of a younger generation on the porch of the Ulupalakua Ranch store. Photo © Randy Jay Braun.

Above: Surrounded by fresh-picked fruit and vegetables, a vendor proudly displays her wares at the weekly Maui Swap Meet in Kahului. Photo @ Douglas Peebles. **Opposite, top left:** Chef James McDonald gauges the readiness of greens for his "fresh from farm to plate" entrees. Photo © Douglas Hoffman. **Top right:** Arriving long ago with Asian immigrants, noodle dishes have become an island staple. Chef Sheldon Simeon samples his. Photo © Douglas Hoffman. **Bottom left:** Bev and Joe Gannon operate high-end restaurants in Hāli'imaile and Wailea, respectively. Photo © Tony Novak-Clifford. **Bottom right:** Chef Marc McDowell peers past the implements of his art in the Mākena Prince hotel kitchen. Photo © Douglas Hoffman.

Above: This whimsical surfboard fence in Ha'ikū has become a tourist favorite and an iconic subject for t-shirts, art photos and even paintings. Photo © Rob DeCamp. **Opposite:** Three generations of stellar musicians gather at a Nāpili slack-key guitar event. From left: Peter de Aquino, Ledward Ka'apana, Richard Ho'opi'i, host George Kahumoku, Jr., Kevin Brown and Sterling Seaton. Photo © Shane Tegarden.

Above: Makawao's annual 4th of July rodeo parade is a great place for island office-seekers to greet crowds of happy voters. Here former mayor Charmaine Tavares of Kula sends a cheerful shaka to the throng. Photo © Randy Hufford. **Opposite:** Among Maui's most iconic events are the midsummer "Obon" dances held on sequential weekends at Japanese and Okinawan Buddhist temples island-wide. All comers are welcome to eat, dance and mingle with friends and family, as at this Lahaina temple. Photo © Rob DeCamp. **Following spread, left:** Renowned Upcountry cowboy Merton Kekiwi displays a hand-worked rawhide rope, a championship buckle, and his rodeo horse at the Oskie Rice Arena in Olinda. Because King Kamehameha was given cattle in the late 1700s by British explorer George Vancouver, Hawai'i had cowboys long before the American West. Photo © Randy Jay Braun. **Following spread, right:** Gowned and garlanded in green, this Kamehameha Day Parade unit of pā'ū riders proudly represents the island of Moloka'i. Photo © Rob DeCamp.

Above: As his peers look on sternly, a daring bull rider blasts out of the chute at the Makawao Rodeo. Held annually over the 4th of July weekend, the venerable rodeo draws Hawai'i's top cowboys and cowgirls for events like barrel racing, bull and bronco riding, calf roping and steer mugging. Photo © Shane Tegarden. **Opposite:** In a blur of speed, two rodeo partners ready their lariats to lasso the head and hoof of a fleeing calf. Over in seconds, the calf roping event requires Swiss watch timing, superlative horses, and impeccable teamwork and accuracy on the part of the ropers. Photo © Ron Dahlquist.

Left: A mixed team of boys and girls from the Nāpili Canoe Club competes in a high school outrigger canoe race in windless waters off Kāʻanapali Beach. Maui canoe clubs coach, equip and sponsor student paddlers from several island high schools. Paddlers must exert maximum effort while maintaining perfect balance, or the canoe will huli (flip). Photo © Rob DeCamp.

Preceding spread: Or should it say "Rumps?" A crew of cowboys and their dog move young pipi (beef cattle) from one pasture to another. In Upcountry Maui, the shortest distance between two meadows is sometimes a state highway. Photo © Ron Dahlquist.

Following spread, left: Maui surfers Inanna Carter and Kai Lenny celebrate his victory in an international paddleboard race. Lenny is also a world-class big wave surfer and board sailor. Photo © Bob Bangerter.

Following spread, right: In an automotive blast from the past, members of the Maui Classic Cruisers Club parade their gleaming chariots through ʻUlupalakua. Photo © Bob Bangerter.

Above: Hawai'i hip-hop sensation Bruno Mars (right) and band member Phillip Lawrence perform for an amped-up crowd at the Maui Arts and Cultural Center in Kahului. Photo © Aubrey Hord. **Opposite:** Legendary British songwriter and recording star Elton John, joined here by bassist Bob Birtch, is among a galaxy of musical luminaries who make the Maui Arts and Cultural Center an essential touring stop. Photo © Aubrey Hord.

Above: One of Upcountry Maui's signature events is the Seabury Hall Crafts Fair. The annual show draws thousands of browsers and buyers to the private school's verdant Olinda campus. Photo © Douglas Peebles. **Opposite:** The Wailea resort has hosted the Maui Film Festival and its galaxy of celebrities for many summers. Here an at capacity festival crowd enjoys a first-run film on an outdoor screen at twilight. Photo © Randy Jay Braun. **Following spread, left:** In his north shore neighborhood, Ha'ikū resident W.S. Merwin is known as the palm tree guy for his backyard palm plantation. Otherwise, he is a U.S. poet laureate and Pulitzer Prize winner. Photo © Tony Novak-Clifford. **Following spread, right:** Hāna's Bully Ho'opai wears many hats: stone mason, evangelical minister, community leader and practitioner of the ancient Hawaiian martial art lua. Photo © Shane Tegarden.

Above: Wearing traditional plantation green paint, Kahakuloa Church is a longtime Christian sentinel on Maui's windy northwest coast. Photo © Rob DeCamp. **Opposite, top left:** Nearing its centennial is Kīhei's picket-fenced Keolahau Congregational Church (1920). Photo © Douglas Peebles. **Opposite, top right:** Erected in 1890, Kaupō's Hui Aloha Church shows classic Hawaiian church style: coral block masonry, whitewashed walls and a rustic wooden steeple. Photo © Douglas Peebles. **Opposite, bottom:** Parishioners and visitors mingle on the lawn following morning services at Mākena's venerable Keawala'i Church (1855). The church is a favorite of South Maui resort guests. Photo © Douglas Peebles.

Above: Maui doesn't produce great musicians by accident. These young barefoot 'ukulele players Tor and Bruno Perez already have fretting and fingering down. Photo © Zach Pezzillo. **Opposite:** The Perez twins strike a winning pose beside a Maui garage. Some island kids swim before they can walk. Photo © Zach Pezzillo.

A baker's dozen of gleaming Harleys forms a proud color guard for a jacaranda grove in full, furious bloom. On a cool spring day, Haleakalā's serpentine, well-banked highway is heaven for bikers. Photo © Randy Jay Braun.

Above: Ballerinas from the Alexander Academy perform a dance sequence from "The Wizard of Oz" at the Maui Theater in Lahaina. Photo © Darrel Wong.
Opposite: Backlit by fiery clouds and a satiny sea, hula dancers tread cool sands at the margin of a Maui day. Photo © David Olsen. **Preceding spread, left:** Two young hula sisters model a classic island couture: feather headbands, Tahitian grass skirts, and blue rubber slippers from Longs. Photo © Randy Jay Braun. **Preceding spread, right:** As Hawai'i's many racial groups and nationalities continue to blend, the face of modern hula looks increasingly like this one: international, multiethnic and focused. Photo © Randy Jay Braun.

Visiting Maui

On June 20, 1866, Mark Twain wrote to his bosses at The Sacramento Union to explain why the paper had not yet received any correspondence from its star reporter. "I went to Maui to stay a week and remained five," Twain explained. "I had a jolly time. I would not have fooled away any of it writing letters under any consideration whatsoever."

Like the millions of visitors who followed him in later decades, Twain found an itinerary already laid out for him. In 1866, this included rolling boulders down into Haleakalā, hiking through 'Īao Valley, and relaxing in sunny Lahaina Town.

These three destinations still top the list 150 years later, but modern Maui visitors also enjoy a greatly expanded itinerary. The island is the same one Twain saw, but it now offers visitors scores of attractions, hundreds of activities and thousands of accommodations. You could even say a visitor's Maui exists alongside the everyday Maui.

The two overlap, of course. Everyone enjoys the same beaches, parks, waterfalls, streams and rainbows. Restaurants and retail stores welcome all, as do the raceways and rodeos. But there is also a subset of Maui experiences crafted chiefly for vacationers.

Consider the way the island is seen. Few residents view Maui from the air, but helicopter tours are a staple of the modern visitor experience. Likewise, many more visitors than islanders see Maui from downhill bicycle seats, zip line harnesses, whale watching boats and parasail slings.

Even when visitors and islanders see the same Maui sights, they do so with different frequency. For instance, vacationers typically

visit Haleakalā, 'Īao Valley, Lahaina, Mākena, Hāna and Kīpahulu in a single week. Unless they were hosting friends from off-island, few residents would complete that circuit in a year.

Ever since Mark Twain popularized guidebooks, Maui visitors have tended to patronize certain well-publicized sites and activities. Mile marker 14 at Olowalu, for instance, is a Mecca for snorkeling tourists, and oncemythic places like Twin Falls, La Pérouse Bay and Venus Pool are now solidly on the map. Travel guides also have helped popularize lū'au shows, Molokini cruises, submarine descents, and window-shopping along Lahaina's Front Street and Baldwin Avenue.

While these attractions are ongoing, Maui also offers what might be called "event tourism." At various times of year, high-profile golf, tennis and basketball tournaments draw legions of off-island fans. Marathons, triathlons, bike races, boardsailing meets and interisland swims, on the other hand, lure active participants. International wine and food expos and a midsummer film festival beckon the glitterati.

Upon arrival, Maui visitors have an array of lodging, dining, shopping, entertainment and recreation choices that would silence even the garrulous Twain. The island's hundreds of hostelries and thousands of stores and restaurants are doubtless well-publicized elsewhere.

Some attractions don't need much publicity. When huge surf is booming, waterfalls are thundering, humpback whales are breaching, or an epic Maui sunset smolders across the sky, everybody pulls over to watch. Then there is only one Maui, and everyone shares it.

Above: Champion fire dancer Ifi So'o plies his dangerous trade for a Maui lū'au audience. Knives, speed, dexterity and flames form a whirling spectacle. Photo © Ron Dahlquist. **Opposite:** Ulua tuna, leopard rays and a shark enthrall viewers at the Maui Ocean Center aquarium in Mā'alaea. At right, bubbles rise from an aquarium worker's regulator. Photo © Greg Vaughn. **Preceding spread:** An early morning beachcomber and a nearby palm tree cast their shadows out onto the ocean at Kā'anapali Beach. Photo © Douglas Peebles.

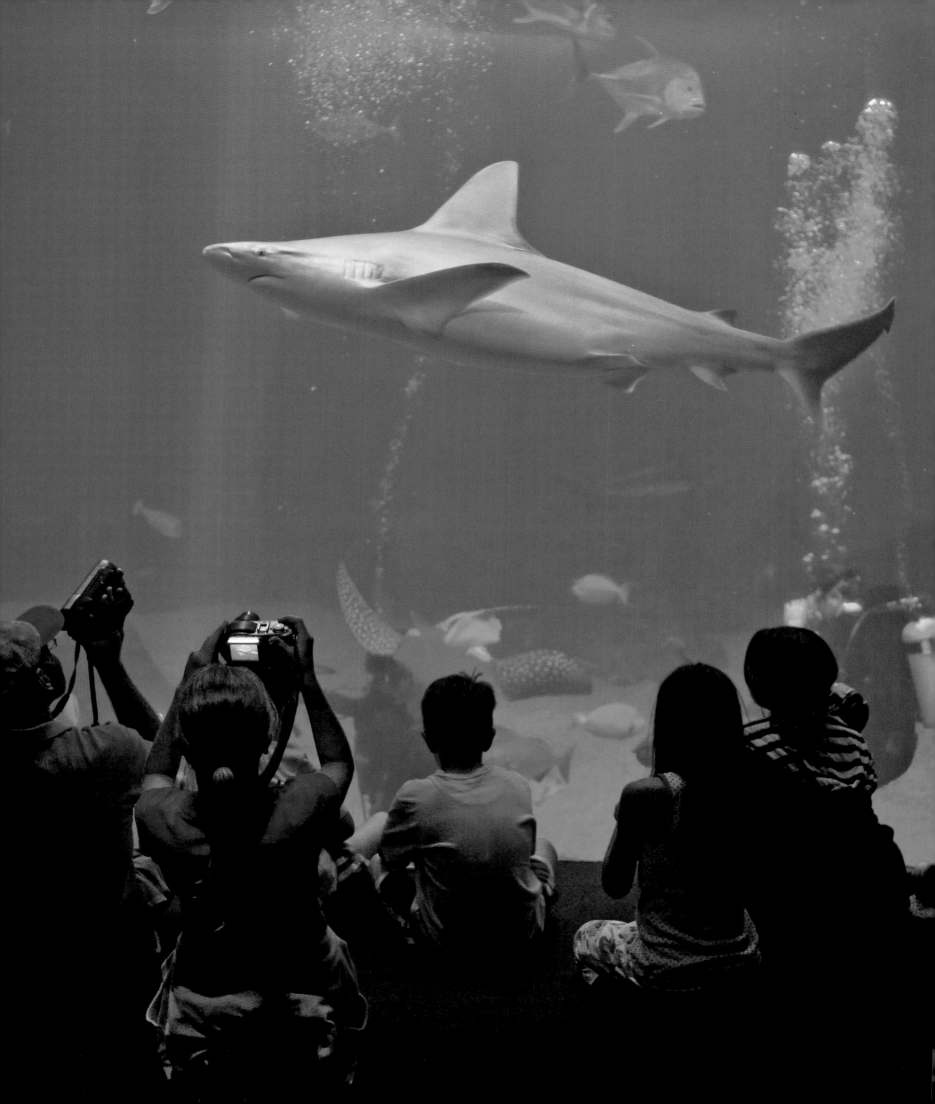

Above: Tutu's Snack Shop on Hāna Bay has earned must-eat status for visitors and islanders alike. Ice cream cones topped this crew's menu. Photo © Ron Dahlquist. **Opposite:** A speeding customer enjoys the Skyline Eco-Adventures zip line ride Upcountry. Zip lines have become a popular visitor thrill at several Maui locations. Photo © Ron Dahlquist.

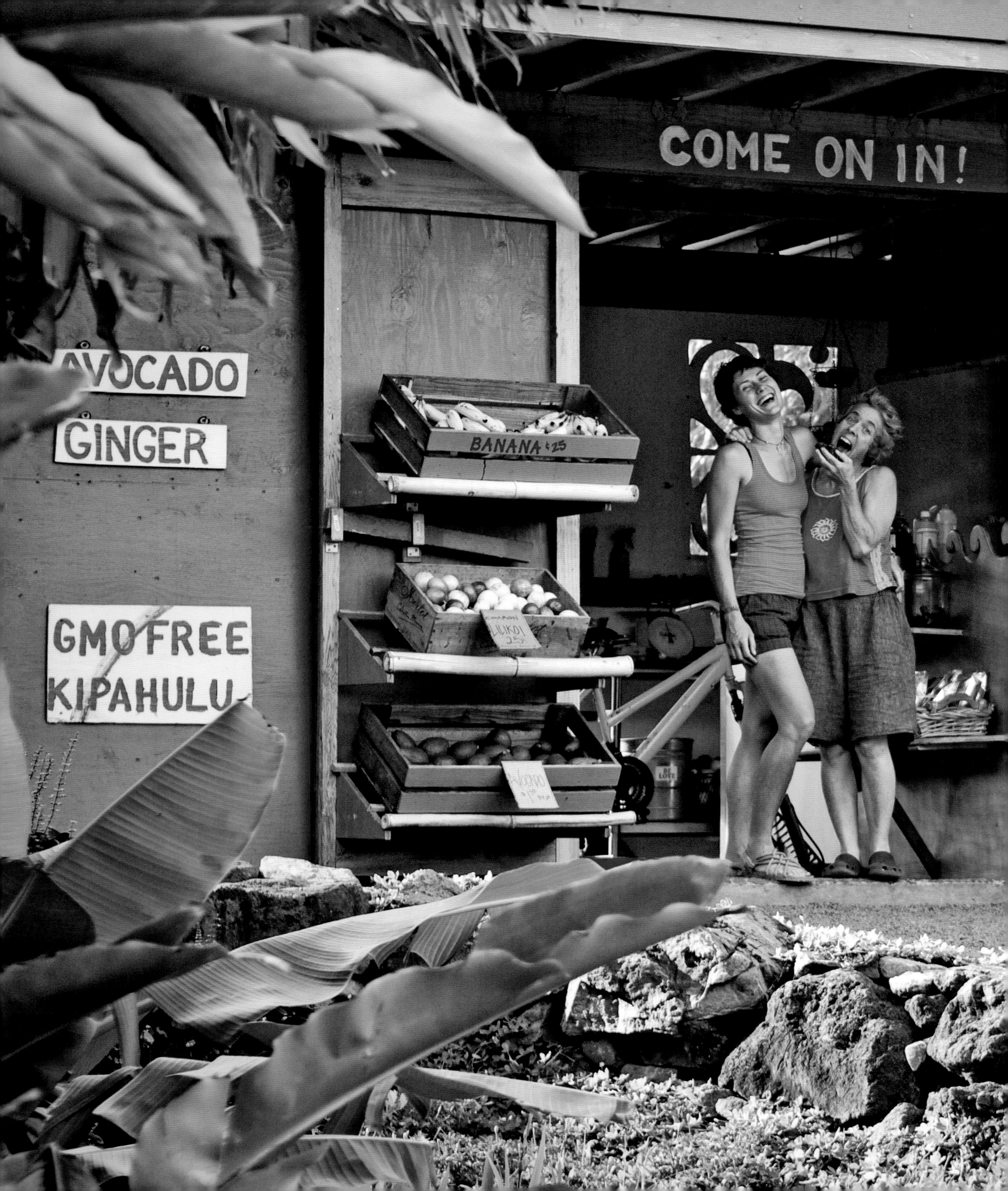
COME ON IN!
AVOCADO
GINGER
GMOFREE
KIPAHULU
BANANA

Right: A guide leads riders down Haleakalā National Park's serpentine Sliding Sands Trail. Private concessionaires run horseback tours, some of which include overnights at soulful cabins built in the 1930s. Photo © Greg Vaughn.

Preceding spread: Best known for its exquisite Seven Pools and famed aviator Charles Lindbergh's grave, remote Kīpahulu also nurtures a thriving organic produce industry. Laughing employees beckon passing motorists to Laulima Farm's roadside stand. Photo © Greg Vaughn.

Following spread, left: Two naiads savor a Polynesian idyll: a plunge in a secluded freshwater pool at the base of a lofty waterfall. This one is Wailua Falls on the Hāna coast. Photo © Greg Vaughn.

Following spread, right: A well-maintained boardwalk gives this hiker an easy transit through an atmospheric bamboo forest in the Kīpahulu section of Haleakalā National Park. Photo © Michael and Monica Sweet.

Right: Downhill bicycle tourists coast past a showy jacaranda tree on a flawless spring morning in Kula. Starting just below the Haleakalā National Park boundary, riders cruise down the mountain at a leisurely pace, rarely having to pedal, letting gravity do the work. Photo © David Olsen.

Preceding spread: The King Kamehameha golf course overlooking Māʻalaea includes majestic views, challenging terrain, and a truly unique clubhouse. Famed architect Frank Lloyd Wright designed this curvaceous complex for film star Marilyn Monroe, but Maui got it instead. Photo © Bob Bangerter.

Left: Visitors enjoy a close encounter with a humpback whale on an unusually serene morning off West Maui. Federal law prohibits whale watching boats from pursuing humpbacks, but the curious leviathans sometimes turn the tables and approach idled boats. This one is doing a spy hop to view its viewers. Photo © Marty Wolff.

Preceding spread, left: A bather savors a blissful moment in one of the freshwater pools dotting the Hāna coast. You don't want to try this on a rainy day, when rocks and branches sometimes plummet over the falls. Photo © Michael and Monica Sweet.

Preceding spread, right: Mile Marker 14 at Olowalu is a longtime snorkeling stop for Maui tourists, who appreciate the site's ease of access, abundant coral, and calm, clear viewing. Photo © Ron Dahlquist.

Above: A seafarer's haven during the whaling era, the lights of Front Street still beckon travelers to Lahaina's oceanfront boutiques, galleries and restaurants. Photo © Randy Hufford. **Following spread:** Twilight shifts the tempo at the Kā'anapali Resort, as vacationers depart the beaches for restaurants, night clubs and lū'au shows. Photo © Douglas Peebles.

Above: Cavorting friends synchronize a leap for the photographer's lens at Wailea Beach. Photo © Linny Morris. **Opposite:** Sunset gently backlights a wedding photographer and his subject on the beach at Kāʻanapali. Seaside weddings have become a Maui tradition and a thriving enterprise. Photo © Douglas Peebles. **Preceding spread:** The torch-lit lūʻau dinner show has been a Hawaiʻi tourist industry fixture for more than a century. Many shows now combine a pan-Polynesian cultural perspective with state-of-the-art technical effects. This Wailea hotel lūʻau show features dances from Sāmoa, Tahiti, Tonga and Hawaiʻi. Photo © David Schoonover.

Above: Watching sunrise gradually gild the sky from the summit of Haleakalā tops the bucket list for many Maui visitors. This group lucked out with crystal clear conditions, although some may have had second thoughts about wearing shorts at 10,000 feet. Photo © Zach Pezzillo.

Future Maui

According to an ancient Hawaiian creation story, the demigod Māui fashioned a hook from a magic bone and went fishing with his brothers. While the others plied their paddles, Māui paid out his sennit line and sent his hook to the ocean floor.

As he felt the magic hook snag the sea bed, Māui ordered his brothers to "huki!" (pull). The mighty paddlers churned the ocean to froth. Gradually the sea floor rose into daylight, and a chain of islands glistened where only trackless ocean had rolled before.

Once humans populated the new islands, Māui's ingenuity was summoned again. The sun sped so swiftly across the sky that fishing nets could not dry. Māui wove a snare from the toughest vines and stole by night to the sun's dwelling place in Haleakalā. As the first rays crept over the summit, Māui netted the sun and held it fast. The sun won release by vowing to cross the heavens more slowly.

Fittingly, the site of Māui's exploits has, in our time, become a nexus of human ingenuity. Atop Haleakalā today, the world's most precise astronomical instruments probe remote galaxies, monitor deep space flights, track satellite and missile launches. One Haleakalā observatory even captures the sun—not with vines, but with futuristic imaging systems.

As Maui moves into the second decade of the challenging 21st Century, the island extends a legacy of innovation that goes all the way back to its namesake. Just as the demigod Māui once captured the sun, modern islanders harness nature's forces for the future.

As carbon-based fuels grow scarcer and costlier to import, Maui has become an optimal site for sustainable energy development. The same robust trade winds that propel Maui

board sailors power wind turbines at Ukumehame on West Maui. Future East Maui wind farms have been penciled in for Nu'u and 'Ulupalakua.

In the ocean, the same swells that thrill Maui surfers have prompted wave energy research on the island's north shore. Another ocean energy project will allow the use of deep sea water to cool Maui buildings. Ocean farming is also being studied, as is desalinization for future water supply.

The sunshine that sustains Maui agriculture and tourism already powers solar collectors island-wide, and photovoltaic arrays are becoming commonplace. Future solar power sources include blue green algae farms that convert sunlight into jet fuel.

None of this happens in a vacuum. In recent years, Maui has developed the infrastructure to support high-level research. The island now has a four-year university campus, a supercomputing center, advanced communications capabilities, and a network of business-government-academic partnerships eager to promote innovation.

These commitments will be tested on this warming planet. As earth's atmosphere grows hotter, wetter and smokier, the oceans will undergo systemic changes as well. Maui in this century will likely see rising sea levels, threats to coral reefs, and alterations to marine habitats, currents and chemistry.

These will be daunting challenges, but Maui can surmount them. The island's namesake, after all, pulled mountains from the sea and slowed the speeding sun. And what he told his brothers still applies today.

To shape the future together, we must "huki!"

Above: The demise of Lahaina's Pioneer Mill sugar plantation opened up prime acreage for other crops, like these specialty coffee beans. Photo © Tony Novak-Clifford. **Opposite:** Workers at Aina Lani Farm in Kula prepare fresh garden herbs for sale to Maui markets and restaurants. Chefs' insistence on fresh, locally grown ingredients has helped diversify island farming. Photo © Linny Morris. **Preceding spread:** Wind turbines climb a West Maui ridge line at Ukumehame. These, and other units planned for East Maui, will ease the island's dependence on imported oil. Photo © Rob DeCamp.

Right: Kula's warm days, cool nights and powdery soil have proved a good fit for strawberries, a fairly recent Maui commercial crop. As sugar, macadamia nuts and pineapple have dwindled, diversified agriculture is gradually gaining traction and market outlets. Photo © Linny Morris.

Preceding spread: Rooftop solar arrays are a fitting power source for the Maui Research and Technology Park, a facility devoted to scientific innovation. Located in Kīhei, the park houses a world-class supercomputer that supports military and university observatories atop Haleakalā. Photo © Shane Tegarden.

The Photographers

BOB BANGERTER has made successful Maui careers in first music, and now photography, focusing on aerials, surfing, nature and fashion. His photography recently won the National Art Competition from the Scottsdale Artists School as well as a Maggie Award nomination.
Website: www.photoimagesmaui.com

RANDY JAY BRAUN arrived in Hawai'i twenty-five years ago as an intern to Kamehameha Schools. After graduation from Occidental College, he and his wife, Anne, opened their own photography and publishing business on Maui. Today Randy owns Hawai'i's oldest fine-art photography gallery. He also leads groups of high-energy photographers on creative adventures throughout the Hawaiian Islands, as well as locations such as Italy and the Alps.
Website: www.randyjaybraun.com

CINDY CAMPBELL'S interest in photography is motivated by the wonder and beauty of the undersea world coupled with her passion for scuba diving. She is continually challenged to master new equipment, techniques and subject matter to keep her work vital and innovative.
Email: Mana61@hawaii.rr.com

RON DAHLQUIST sold his first photographs to a small surf magazine over 40 years ago. He has since shot numerous sports and worldwide travel locations for a long list of clients. Maui, however, remains his favorite place in the world to live and to shoot.
Website: www.rondahlquist.com

ROB DECAMP is continually inspired by the world's diversity and color. Capturing Hawai'i's ever changing beauty from the fiery volcano of the Big Island to the rainforests of Kaua'i, excites him most about photography.
Email: photorob@aol.com

QUINCY DEIN grew up on Maui, which gifted him with a deep appreciation for adventure, the outdoors, and the ocean. When not behind the lens, he enjoys surfing, diving, kite boarding, hiking, and traveling.
Website: www.quincydein.com

TERRIE ELIKER: After 30 years in newspaper production, Terrie left to become her own boss. In addition to photography and graphic design, she is the director of the Maui Photo Festival & Workshops.
Website: www.mauiphotofestival.com

DAVID FLEETHAM'S photographs have been published worldwide in tens of thousands of magazines, books and calendars, and have been featured on over two hundred magazine covers, which includes the only underwater image ever to appear on the cover of LIFE. His award-winning work has been published by National Geographic, The Cousteau Society, the Discovery Channel, and the BBC.
Website: www.davidfleetham.com

ANITA HARRIS is an enthusiastic photographer and Photoshop specialist who lives in the UK but favors Maui for its unique land and ocean photographic opportunities, its unusual lighting conditions and rare wildlife. She is also a designer of photography websites.
Website: www.anitaharris.com

DOUGLAS J. HOFFMAN is living his dream creating portraits, resort decor, and being the featured artist in a Front Street gallery. He also organizes workshops and travel photography adventures.
Website: www.douglasjhoffman.com

AUBREY HORD is a world traveler known for her mastery of light, movement, vivid colors and designs. She is a Teaching Artist at the Hui No'eau Visual Arts Center as well as Award-winning Maui celebrity portrait and wedding photographer.
Website: www.aubreyhord.com

RANDY HUFFORD is in awe of the beauty of Maui which has captured his heart. His inspiration comes from God who opens his eyes to see the wonder of His creation. Randy's goal is to create images that invoke peace, joy and healing.
Website: www.RandyHuffordArt.com

LEAH MARK, born and raised in Pacific Grove, California, has lived her life through the lens. Since moving to Maui she is a four-time award winner of the Maui Photo Festival including 2010 Best Overall and 2009 Best Wildlife.
Email: leahkmark@yahoo.com

LAURENT MARTRES is the author of four highly-praised books: *Land of the Canyons* and three volumes for the *Photographing the Southwest* series and has published several himself. Photography enthusiasts from around the world enjoy his books and are inspired by his images.
Website: www.martres.com

SCOTT MEAD'S grandfather, during a Hawai'i family vacation in 1974, presented him with a Kodak Instamatic camera, a hand full of film cartridges, and told him to have fun. Mead is still having fun today, trudging deep into bamboo forests, climbing lava, and hanging out of helicopters to capture some of Hawai'i's most dramatic landscapes.
Website: www.scottmeadphotography.com

LINNY MORRIS has been photographing professionally for over 30 years. She enjoys the variety inherent in what can loosely be called lifestyle photography, which encompasses relaxed portraits, travel, food, interiors, architecture and still-life. In other words, she specializes in not specializing.
Website: www.linnymorris.com

MIKE NEAL came to Maui in 1973 to surf big waves where it was love at first sight. He is enamored by Maui's natural beauty from the ocean to the top of Haleakalā. Photographs allow him to capture and share many rare moments in time.
Website: www.NealStudios.net

CAMERON NELSON has traveled the globe for the past two decades to capture a mesmerizing blend of nature-inspired imagery. His passion and love for adventure are the motivating forces behind his photography.
Website: www.cameronnelsongallery.com

Background: Mā'alea Beach. Photo © Zach Pezzillo.
Following page, background: Photo © David Olsen.

*M*aui is a visual change artist that provides a myriad of options in terms of capturing striking landscapes, shifting light, vivid colors, clear blue water, majestic mountains and waterfalls that ebb and flow with the seasons. Each day brings something new in terms of light and shadows, and the subtle changes provide incredible opportunities for photographers. (Aubrey Hord)

It is a magical island, filled with inspiration, grace, and beauty (David Watersun) that inspires creativity and passion. Whether it's big surf, native birds, the awesome beauty of a sunset or the crystal blue underwater, Maui provides breathtaking and rare moments to capture. (Mike Neal)

Photographing the island is like opening the front door and finding yourself in the Land of Oz. (Shane Tegarden) The spirit, or mana, that the Island possesses, found within the ever-changing luminosity of light, the fluidity and motion of the sea and the diversity of the ʻāina enables Maui's essence to be captured through the lens. (Scott Mead) Most awesome are the constantly changing light and shapes. The wind is almost always blowing and the ocean, skies, sand and creatures always moving, creating a huge variety of endless opportunities to be captured. (Marty Wolfe)

—Interpolation of photographers' quotes

TONY NOVAK-CLIFFORD has called Maui home for three decades, producing award-winning advertising campaigns and editorial spreads for clients worldwide. He finds Maui's quality of light magical—a photographer's dream.
Website: www.tonynovak-clifford.com

DAVID OLSEN grew up in Southern California, but moved to Maui in the late seventies. He attended Brooks Institute of Photography where he received a degree in Commercial Photography.
Website: www.davidolsen.com

DOUGLAS PEEBLES has been photographing Hawaiʻi and the South Pacific for over 30 years. His work can be seen in magazines, calendars and in over 50 books on Hawaiʻi.
Website: www.douglaspeebles.com

ZACH PEZZILLO was raised on Maui and enjoys photographing nature and people. At only 17 years of age, he has received local and national recognition for his photography and has accumulated numerous awards. His photographs have appeared in juried competitions, books, and magazines.
Website: www.redbubble.com/people/zpezzillo

DAVE SCHOONOVER has been working behind a camera for 45 years. A retired firefighter, he started a full-time photo business in 2009 that specializes in landscape and nature photography. Besides an extensive Hawaiʻi portfolio, he travels and photographs California and the National Parks of the West.
Email: dsphotomaui@gmail.com

MONICA AND MICHAEL SWEET express themselves as a team that spends its days doing what they truly love: traveling and photographing the Hawaiian Islands. Between them they have won over 20 international awards for excellence.
Website: www.gallerysweet.com

SHANE TEGARDEN lives in Kīhei, Hawaiʻi and has been photographing the beauty of Maui for over thirty years. Love of the island and its people are the inspirations behind his images.
Website: www.stphotography.com

GREG VAUGHN, a former twenty-year Hawaiʻi resident, is now an editorial and commercial photographer based in Eugene, Oregon. He specializes in recreational travel, scenic landscape and nature photography. He is the principal photographer for several Fodor's Compass American Guide books and the author and photographer for the guidebook Photographing Oregon.
Website: www.GregVaughn.com

JESSICA VELTRI fell in love with the beauty of Hawaiʻi and the art of photography while she was stationed in the islands for a military assignment. A veteran of Iraq and Afghanistan, she enjoys traveling with camera in tow to capture the places and people she encounters along the way. She was recently reassigned to the east coast and while the army will continue to take her around the world, Hawaiʻi will always be in her heart and on her mind.
Website: www.jessicaveltri.com

DAVID WATERSUN has photographed Maui's people, places, and lifestyle for several decades creating editorial, advertising, and corporate images for print and online media usage. He has also photographed for several books about Maui: *The Maui Chef Seafood Cookbook, Under a Maui Roof,* and *Kapalua Nui: Place Of Life.*
Email: watersun@maui.net

FRANK WICKER spends many hours inside Haleakalā capturing the play of natural light on the distinctive shapes and forms of the landscape, which drives his quest to capture the emotional appeal of the natural world.
Website: www.wicker.photoshelter.com

MARTY WOLFF, a Bronx born Baby Boomer, has always loved photography, especially as an artform. He lives his dream in Maui and travels Hawaiʻi and the world seeking that truth— "Beyond the initial image is a more mysterious truth."
Website: www.martywolff.com

DARRELL WONG grew up in Kapahulu on Oʻahu. He has a wonderful family, loves what he does and works with fantastic people on really amazing jobs in one of the most incredibly beautiful places on Earth.
Website: www.darrellwong.com

Suggested Reading

Ariyoshi, Rita. *Maui On My Mind*. Honolulu: Mutual Publishing, 1988.

Bartholomew, Gail, and Bren Bailey. *Maui Remembers*. Honolulu: Mutual Publishing, 1994.

Clark, John R. K. *The Beaches of Maui County*. Honolulu: University of Hawai'i Press, 1980.

Engledow, Jill. *Exploring Historic Upcountry*. Honolulu: Watermark Publishing, 2001.

Fiene-Severns, Pauline, and Mike Severns. *Molokini: Hawaii's Island Sanctuary*. Honolulu: Island Heritage Publishing, 2002.

Forestell, Paul H., and Gregory Dean Kaufman. *Humpbacks of Hawai'i: The Long Journey Back*. Waipahu: Island Heritage Publishing, 2008.

Goldsberry, Steven. *Maui the Demigod: An Epic Novel of Mythical Hawaii*. Honolulu: University of Hawai'i Press, 1989.

Hamilton, Peter Freeland. *The Man Who Loved Lahaina : George Freeland, Founder of the Pioneer Inn, Lahaina, Maui, Hawaiian Islands: His Life and Times*. San Mateo: Peter F. Hamilton Co., 2001.

Harden, M.J. *Voices of Wisdom: Hawaiian Elders Speak*. Kula: Aka Press, 1999.

Hoover, John P. *Hawai'i's Fishes: A Guide for Snorkelers and Divers*. 2nd ed. Honolulu: Mutual Publishing, 2007.

James, Van. *Ancient Sites of Maui, Moloka'i and Lāna'i*. Honolulu: Mutual Publishing, 2002.

Kepler, Angela Kay. *Maui's Hana Highway, a Visitor's Guide*. Honolulu: Mutual Publishing, 1995.

Maui's Floral Splendor. Honolulu: Mutual Publishing, 1995.

Sunny South Maui: A Guide to Kihei, Wailea and Makena. Honolulu: Mutual Publishing, 199

Wonderful West Maui: A Guide to Lahaina, Kaanapali, Kapalua, and Iao Valley. Honolulu: Mutual Publishing, 1992.

Kyselka, Will, and Ray Lanterman. *Maui: How It Came To Be*. Honolulu: University of Hawai'i Press, 1980.

Liittschwager, David, and Susan Middleton. *Remains of a Rainbow: Rare Plants and Animals of Hawai'i*. Washington, D.C.: National Geographic, 2001.

The Maui News, 1900-2000 : 100 Years as Maui's Newspaper. Wailuku: Maui News, 2000.

Max, Blue, Charlie Lyons, and Leslie Lyons. *Jaws Maui*. Waialua: Maui Ltd., 1997.

Peebles, Douglas. *From the Skies of Paradise: Maui*. Honolulu: Mutual Publishing, 1992.

Pratt, H. Douglas, and Jacob Faust. *Enjoying Birds and Other Wildlife in Hawai'i: A Site-by-Site Guide to the Islands for the Birder and Naturalist*. 3rd Ed. Honolulu: Mutual Publishing, 1993.

Sinclair, Marjorie. *The Wild Wind: A Love Story of Old Maui*. Honolulu: Mutual Publishing, 1987.

Speakman, Cummins E., Jr. *Mowee: A History of Maui the Magic Isle*. Edited by Jill Engledow. Honolulu: Mutual Publishing, 2001.

Sterling, Elspeth P. *Sites of Maui*. Honolulu: Bishop Museum Press, 1998.

Stevens, Tom. *Maui Bound*. Edited by Betty Fullard-Leo. Honolulu: Pacific Islands Publishing, Ltd., 1991.

Von Tempski, Armine. *Born in Paradise*. Woodbridge, CT: Ox Bow Press, 1985.

Wenkam, Robert. *Maui: The Last Hawaiian Place*. Edited by Kenneth Brower. New York: McCall Publishing Co., 1970.

Maui: No Ka Oi. Chicago: Rand McNally, 1980.